Chasing the

Money

A True-Life Story of Insurance Fraud

Dan Cupaiuolo

DISCLAIMER:

This publication is based on real occurrences as experienced and told by the writer/author. All information regarding the events that have taken place is from the author's perspective. Names, places, and some details have been altered to protect the privacy of others who may have been involved. Neither the writer, author nor publisher are responsible for any consequences that may result from the events told in this publication.

Acknowledgement

To my kids: I would do anything to see you guys with good careers, making the most of yourselves that you can. Don't take anything for granted. Work hard, legitimately, and God will reward you with good.

Introduction

There's a scripture in the Bible that says people judge by outer appearances, but God sees the heart. Sometimes we see the materialistic things in this world, and we think that's our goal. That's the endgame. The "American Dream" sort of speak. But, looking back, I think 'at what cost?' Looking back on the things I've seen and done, and the consequences of it all, I ask myself if it was worth it.

To this day, people don't understand why I did what I did. Sometimes, it's hard for even me to understand it. But I'll tell you this, it happened for a reason. No one knows what they're capable of until you find yourself in a "back against the wall" situation. It's easy to look at someone else's dirt and say you'd never do what they did. But when you're exposed to a "lifestyles of the rich and famous" environment, it's easy to fill your eyes with it and get caught up in the façade. There's a phrase my pastor says every week after church service. He says, "Who you hang out with is who you become." That's exactly right. I was hanging around the wrong crowd, the Chasers; and before I knew it, I became one of them.

In my mind, I just wanted to give my family the best life I could. I wanted to provide for them and give them more than what they needed. And, I'm not excusing what I did or blaming them. I take and have taken full responsibility for my actions. All I'm saying is that my family is everything to me, and at the time, I made a huge mistake in thinking this was the only and best way to provide. A mistake I'm still paying for today.

Now, you see all these commercials against insurance fraud and what the consequences are when you commit fraud. I can tell you the commercials don't do it justice. Insurance fraud is a federal offense. The consequences are far worse than they let off. I can only thank God for His grace and mercy. But there was a time when the insurance company was the bank and cars were atm cards. What you're going to read might seem unbelievable and a bit fabricated. But it's a true story. A story I couldn't possibly make up because I lived it firsthand.

Chapter 1 – Living the High Life

It was 1956 in South Philadelphia, the year Elvis Presley had his first hit "Heartbreak Hotel," Rocky Marciano retired as the undefeated Heavyweight Champion of the world, and the average cost of a brand-new car was only $2000. But, in South Philly, Dante and Agnes Cupaiuolo were just a married couple living in their old two-story brick townhouse raising their 6 children as a young family. I, Dan Cupaiolo, was the second oldest of my siblings.

My father, Dante, was a hard-working man; a real provider for our home. I guess you can say he was a "jack of all trades." He did all kinds of different jobs; masonry and construction work, car sales, and music. Music was his passion, though. He was a great musician, and that's where he made most of his money. He landed a deal with the U.S. Government, which required him to travel around the world to perform at all the NCO clubs for the U.S. military. The pay was great, he was able to provide for us but at a cost. Not being home because of his travel schedule took a toll on his marriage and on our family.

I was 11 years-old when my parents got divorced. At first, we lived with my mother. It was fine for a few years until she met a new man. When he moved in, it seemed like she was, suddenly, tired of us kids; like she was tired of taking care of us. Her new guy moved into our house and started treating us like his little slaves. He was a complete jerk. I can't tell you the number of times I'd imagine myself socking him in the face.

Now, my mother worked as a waitress at a well-known restaurant in Philly. She worked all kinds of shifts, especially nights. So, most days, she slept in late; and, I would often hide in the attic and cut school. She never noticed and it was working just fine until one day I nearly killed her! While she was asleep upstairs in her room, I was hiding in the closet downstairs and playing with some matches I'd found in the kitchen. Well, I lit the house on fire! My brothers and I ran up the stairs, woke my mom up, and got out of the house just in time. I'm glad everyone got out alive, but my mother had had enough. She was tired of watching us and gave my dad full custody.

I guess it worked out for the best, either way, my dad didn't like the fact that another man was living in the house with us and bossing us around, making us go to the store and buy his beer. So, he bought a house across the bridge in New Jersey. Moving to Jersey was great. It was nothing like Philadelphia. There was much less crime, less traffic, less congestion; and, back then, it was mostly farmland. There was a lot more room for us in the house. My father was, also, living with one of his employees, Jackie. She was half his age, but she took pretty good care of us.

By this time, my dad was able to be home much more. He didn't have to travel as much because he was booking different bands all over the world and getting paid very well by the government. He got into buying and reselling properties and, after school, I would help him with the remodeling of his houses. Soon, he was buying gas stations, drug stores, hair salons; all types of properties that he could fix and flip. He was an incredible businessman, and I wanted to be just like him.

Eventually, he purchased a three-acre lot and scored a contract to build what, back then, was the largest auto body shop in South Jersey. During construction, the shop owner offered me a job. So, when the shop was finished, I started working there, learning the trade, and detailing cars. Then, I moved from prep person to paint, to body man. I was a fast learner and exceptionally good at what I did. This is how it all started for me in the auto body business. The more I did it, the more I loved what I did.

My father saw how profitable the collision business was and decided to build his own auto body shop. And, thankfully, it was a very successful business for him. The shop allowed him the time to raise his kids and, with the money he was making, he bought about 27 other properties. No doubt, back then, the collision business was ridiculously lucrative. Who wouldn't want to cash in? And, I have to give my dad credit. The man had never worked on a car in his life, but he learned the business and administrative part of it and made it work.

God bless that man; he could do anything. My father was (as the young folks say) the real "O.G." and I was blessed to have him in my life. Three years later, my father met one of his old friends from Philly. His friend was deep in the mob over there but started hanging around the shop more often. He was buying wrecked cars and paying my father big money to fix them up. This kept the shop busy and made my dad a lot of money. Next thing you know, more mobsters started coming around the shop. I may have been young at the time, but I was smart enough to figure out what was going on. Eventually, we had everyone coming in, from pimps to drug dealers. I never asked any questions. They did what they had to do in those days. And, unlike today, back in those days, there was a "loyalty" factor. Everyone made money and everyone looked out for each other.

I spent a total of 20 years in that shop with my father. I was raised believing that family came first, and you should stay by your dad's side. But I did take a four-year break to go work in the casino business in Atlantic City. Those were different times back then, too. I started as a dealer and was soon promoted to a floor person in the craps pit. Now, the year was 1979, and the casino business was great. Casino employees got free tuxedos, food, and the opportunity to hang with celebrities. We just couldn't gamble in the casino. At first, I started as a dice dealer, but my dad had connections. Soon, I was (as we called it then) "juiced" into a Supervisor's position. I couldn't have asked for a better gig. But, if I did, I probably would've gotten it. My dad was a "big player" in those days.

But it seemed like, no matter what I did, I was always led back to the body shop. It was my gift and my curse! One of the owners of the casino had his metallic grey Mercedes 2-seater shipped from Las Vegas. Unfortunately, he was in an accident and knew that my dad owned a shop. So, he had his car towed there for repairs and wanted to change the color to a bright orange red. Well, I took on the task of removing every part of the vehicle. Lights, molding, trim, bumpers; you name it. I painted this Mercedes inside and out – it was perfect! I, personally, delivered the car to the casino owner. This guy couldn't believe his eyes. He inspected it carefully, and loved it so much, he promoted me again!

He was my protection! I was completely untouchable, and everyone knew it. Every employee knew he was my "juice," and no one asked questions. They knew it was always best to mind their own business. A year later, though, he was denied his permanent gambling license. It seems this guy was heavily involved in organized crime, and he was sent back to Las Vegas. With his absence, it wasn't long before the Philly Crew that worked with him started pushing pounds of powder on me. They needed me to move it for them. I guess they figured, since I was working night shift, I could do that. Everyone needed something more than caffeine to keep them going through the night. I never used it, but I'll tell you those drugs moved quick.

Before I knew it, the money was coming in hard and fast. I didn't know where to hide it all. But, trust me, a young guy exposed to the high life; I found a way. There's nothing quite like wearing $1000 designer suits and shoes ranging anywhere from $800 to $1500. I lived in a very nice apartment in Brigantine, exactly a block and a half from the beach. I had everything a 23-year-old ever wanted and more than I needed. My self-made dreams come true. But all that glitz and glam of the Casino wouldn't last for long.

Chapter 2 – Back to Shop

One Friday night, my friend Jimmy calls me up to hang out. We were gambling in the casino and hit about $15,000. It was getting pretty late, so I asked the pit boss, who was also a friend of mine, for a comped room and dinner. You might not know what that means, but basically when a room is comped to you, it's given at no charge. I hooked my friend up with the comped room since I only lived three miles away. Jimmy went to his room and I went home. All was good and well when I left. Or, so I thought.

Unfortunately, the next morning, my idiot friend got arrested for possession of drugs found in the room. He, then, tells the Casino Control Commission this whole elaborate story about us gambling, that I was a casino employee and I had won that money. Jimmy also sold out my pit boss friend for the free room and dinner. The pit boss got written up, and they called me to the office. When they confronted me, of course, I denied it all, but they believed Jimmy. I had no choice but to resign, since they didn't have enough evidence to fire me. The Commission suspended my casino license so I couldn't work at any other casino. And, back then, whatever they said went. It took me ten years to get my license back. What could I do?

I went back to what I knew best; I was back in the shop. And, my father welcomed me with open arms. A few years later, my dad was tired of the upkeep and maintenance required to run the body shop; so, he decided to sell. He got a large cash offer from a drug dealer who needed a business front for his real business. He also got rid of most of his properties, going down from 27 to only 4. He couldn't wait to get as far away as he could from Atlantic City tax and Jersey altogether. He sold his house, took the cash, and moved to Florida.

The guy who bought my dad's shop offered me a job there. He needed me to stay there and keep things running like normal in order to avoid suspicion. It was strange, though, he only came around maybe once every two weeks. He'd stop by, say hello, and then leave. Every Friday, his father-in-law would come by to do payroll and sign the vendor checks. But he'd leave right after. It was like I ran my own business most of the time, but that would soon end.

They invited me over to their house for dinner and proceeded to tell me that some people were looking for them. They wanted to kill them and their family, so they were going to disappear and asked me to keep the shop running as long as I could. As it turns out, they had turned on a couple of big players and went under witness protection. The shop remained open for another three months until the state came in and closed it down.

Right around this time, I had connected with the love of my life. I swear she was the most beautiful girl I'd ever met. She was beautiful, and still is. We may not be together now, but she's still the most beautiful person I've ever met inside and out; hardworking, God-fearing, Christ-loving woman.

We, initially, met at the casino while she was still working there. But she wanted nothing to do with me when we were working in the casino together. I had a bit of a reputation and I had a lot going on back then. I was a young guy, not too bad looking, and I had a lot of girls around me all the time. So, of course, there was no way she wanted to get involved with me. But, as fate would have it, one day she had a slight problem with the paint on her car. She knew I was still in the auto body business, so she looked me up and asked me to repaint her car. Now, her car was only two years old, but when I got done with it, it looked brand new. She was excited to see how good it looked. The expression on her face said it all, and I took my chance right there. I said, "Now, we gotta go out to dinner." She accepted, one thing led to another, and I knew she was the woman I was going to marry.

We dated for about five years after that. I felt I had found the love of my life. Eventually, she left the casino and started going to school to pursue her dreams. We got married in 1987, I'll never forget it. We rented out a nice venue in Bellmawr, NJ. There were a couple hundred people at our wedding. And, all I could think was that I had found my perfect fit. Nothing like getting to spend the rest of your life with that special person.

God blessed us with three beautiful children and a very nice home in Washington Township, NJ, which I built for my wife and kids. She had to take a few years off from school to raise our kids, but when they became teenagers, she went back to school. This woman was amazing, didn't even miss a beat. She reached her goal and got her degree, just like she wanted. We had 3 of the greatest kids in the world; two boys and our beautiful daughter. We made sure they attended the best schools, and they each excelled in their classes. We were truly blessed as parents, and we couldn't have been prouder of our kids.

But, while she was in school, I was going from job to job; always trying to get ahead to support my family and my wife while she was getting her degree. I would do anything to make sure my family had everything they needed, the best I could! Maybe that was the problem. Maybe I let my desire to give my family everything get out of hand. Or, maybe it was me getting tired of and tangled up in the ruthlessness of the auto body shop business. I mean, shop owners were some of the greediest people I'd ever known. They had no problem working the hell out of you and paying you well under the amount of work you did. I was working 70-80 hours a week because that was the only way I could make the money I needed for us to live.

Then, I found a shop in Philadelphia that was paying a lot more than the one I worked at in Jersey. I thought this was my big break, so I took a shot to cross the bridge and start over at that body shop. My plan was to work there until I found a better paying auto body repair shop closer to home. That was my plan, but life had other plans. I only wish I could've seen it coming.

Chapter 3 – Crossing the Bridge

From here on out, everything that has happened to me has been a direct result of one little seemingly harmless decision. When I crossed that bridge to work at a body shop in Philadelphia, things changed drastically; and not just for me, but also for my family. The pay was better and there was plenty of work, things were starting to come together. And, then I met Joey Maldonado, the owner of one of the largest shops in Philly – Moe's Collision. His shop was huge in work and in size; with over 40 employees, the shop was a little larger than an entire city block and raked in about two million dollars a month. They had so much work, in fact, that they had to send some to me.

This shop was incredible. Even though they had their own trucks, they had 14 other tow truck drivers bringing them cars. It was a twenty-four-hour shop, so they would get work constantly. They got cars in from everywhere, not just their trucks and outside tow truck drivers. People were bringing cars to Moe's Collision because the commission was better. I didn't see this kind of stuff in Jersey, but the more time I spent working in the city, the more I understood why Moe's Collision was a money pit.

It was in crossing the bridge that I discovered who they were. Chasers. They were tow truck drivers, better known as "accident chasers," which is how they got their name. They'd sit in their trucks all day and well into the night in different areas of the city; listening on their scanners for any nearby car crashes. When they heard something on the scanner, they'd race over to the accident and offer to tow the cars to their auto repair shops. Their sole job was to sit in the trucks and wait. To this day, the city is filled with these Chasers competing for work, rushing to the scene of any accident, trying to get clients locked in with them. Many of them offered promises of kickbacks and savings on deductibles; they'd hand out business cards for certain lawyers and doctors they did business with. It was a "crash and cash" ring. Yes, the body shop business was different in the city, night and day compared to Jersey.

Sometime after we met, Joey Maldonado offered me a job managing his shop. I couldn't believe it; this was the opportunity of a lifetime. I was going to manage this city block wide, multi-million-dollar building decked out with all the employees and equipment needed to make even more money. Most shop owners would kill to have even half of Moe's Collision's business; and I was going to be in charge of it. Life couldn't get any better. Soon, Joey was making so much money, he started a construction business on the side. His time was pretty divided, most of it going to the construction business, so I took care of almost everything at the shop. I was making money and my family had more than they needed. Yup, crossing the bridge was the best decision I had made so far (at least, that's what I thought).

Now, the chasing business certainly ran differently across the bridge, and has since changed a number of ways. But some politicians had caught wind of the business and the competitive nature of accident chasers, and they wanted to be a part of the profit receiving end. So, when it came to towing cars for illegal street parking violations, the city had no interest in purchasing their own trucks – it was too costly. No, they came up with something better and more profitable for the city.

They started a "rotated" towing system in which they'd choose tow trucks, body shops and tow yards and assign them with a week of the month to handle any towing/stowing needs for the city. Those picked would get all the tows for their assigned area for that week. Then, everyone would be on a rotating schedule. This was done, of course, for a fee. "Organized towing" was making the city money along with the businesses chosen. But there were still "independent" chasers who refused to pay the fee. So, they'd steal tows here and there because they knew, if they didn't get caught, the reward would be worth it. Currently, the city has slowed the "chasing" business down, but shady things still go on from time to time. Some chasers are just willing to keep taking risks.

Chapter 4 – The Chasers

Every Chaser in the area knew "Joey Mal," that's what they called him in the city. They knew that, if you wanted the best commission on a wreck, Joey Mal was the guy to bring it to. Twenty percent of the insurance estimate to be exact! So, if someone brought a $10,000 job, that Chaser would make $2000 in commission plus the tow money. The most experienced Chaser was pulling in $8000 to $9000 a week! That's close to $40-grand a month! Imagine making that kind of money. No wonder this was all they did, everyday; twenty-four seven.

Police scanners were their lifelines. Every time they heard of an accident over the radio, they'd get an exact location on the hit. They were so clever sometimes the Chasers would work in crews. This gave them the advantage of getting to the crash scene faster because they were able to cover more ground. The drivers would race and there would be 2, sometimes 4, tow trucks at one location. After a while, it just got ridiculous. There would be fist fights and even shootings, all over who would get the tow!

When the cops started getting involved, things changed a little bit. It got somewhat better. It was more territorial, and the teams would split up and only work certain areas of the city. But they all knew not to cross over into another Chaser's territory. There was an understanding, now, and mutual respect among the Chasers. There was a lot less fighting over jobs because they respected each other's turf.

I knew every single one of these Chasers, their nicknames and their trucks. There were a lot we dealt with back then; Rover, Worm-man, Otto, Triple Steel, Junior, to name a few. And, they all wrapped their trucks with big, bold, and bright-colored letters. There was no way you could miss them on the street! As the manager at Moe's Collision, they depended on me to get the most dollars I could out of every job they brought. I earned their respect quickly because I understood that they were commission-based, and the more I squeezed out of insurance companies, the more they made…the more I made.

Running the shop operations was one thing, but my main and most important job was keeping the Chasers happy. They brought in all the work, and if they weren't happy, no one would be. If we shorted them or paid them the wrong commission, we wouldn't get work for weeks from them. They'd take the jobs to other shops until everything was straightened out and all was cool again. There was no "I.O.U." in a Chaser's vocabulary. It just didn't happen. They were merciless about their money, after all, it was their livelihood; it was all they knew.

For the most part, this was the only gig the Chasers had; except for one. Chris was a chaser who also dealt crack cocaine. Towing cars was a front, and he'd drive around mostly at night dealing bags of all sizes filled with drugs. No one, especially not the police, was going to suspect that a tow truck driver would be dealing drugs out of his truck. In fact, the police got along with him because, if there was an accident, he was fast on the scene to clear it up. And, this would avoid causing traffic on the roads. He did a good job putting up a front with his truck.

Chris made more money than any other Chaser in the city of Philadelphia. In fact, he'd clear $15,000 to $30,000 a week from his drug sales. Chris made serious money, but he had one serious defect – he was always flaunting his cash. It was almost like he was inviting people to rob him! Everyone (the shady folks & drug addicts) knew what he was into, and this was not good. One night, one of his "clients" kidnapped Chris' 12-year-old brother. The drug addict threatened to kill Chris' little brother if Chris didn't give him $300,000. And, they knew he couldn't call the police because it was dirty money. They had also warned him that even if he decided to come clean and tell the cops, they'd make sure he never saw the kid again.

So, Chris paid the $300,000 ransom and saved his brother's life. He also stopped dealing drugs and stuck to strictly chasing. He still complains about the amount of money he makes now compared to when he dealt drugs, but he also says no amount of cash is worth the risk of losing a loved one. Lesson learned, I guess.

These guys…the chasers; they all depend on the chase. But I'll never forget the time we did end up shortening their commission – it was a complete nightmare. Joey Mal's construction business needed money to fund a project, and he decided to take it from the shop. On any other occasion, this wouldn't have been an issue. Except that one day a week, all jobs would be written, and all the drivers would be paid on that same day. The Chasers always wanted their money after the estimate was written and before the job on the vehicle was completed. Well, that was the day Joey needed the money, and if there's one brutal lesson I got that day, it was not to mess with a Chaser's money. They were pissed that they had to wait to get paid, so they started taking their jobs to other shops, which in turn, affected me!

So, my salary was also being affected by the construction company's needs. I was owed over $5000 in commission. Everything that was coming into the shop was going into the construction company, constantly. The construction company was killing Joey's body shop business. The Chasers were using his trucks but taking the jobs to other shops because he wasn't paying them. There wasn't much for the shop, and I'm no genius, but that didn't make much business sense to me. One day, one of the unhappy drivers came up to me and started talking to me about another shop in Northeast Philly. He told me the owner was looking for a manager to turn the shop around and he was willing to pay whatever it took to make it happen. I thought the timing might be perfect to take a drive to the shop and meet up with the owner.

One decision after another, and I had no idea where it was leading me to because all I could think about was the money factor. Life is truly a product of our choices, and if we make the wrong ones or don't consult with God, it will inevitably lead to disaster. I couldn't see past the "green," and that was my first mistake.

Chapter 5 – Making the Money

Moe's was where I started seeing the "green pastures" if you know what I mean. There were many times, when vehicles came in, that the car damage was minimal. So, if it was a newer vehicle and higher in value, we'd take it and run it into a pole outside the shop. One time, someone brought in a brand-new Lexus GX (an SUV) into the shop. But the damage on it was minor, so we took the car and backed it into the shop and into the frame machine. The body man hit the frame machine so hard, the car pushed through to the shop's overhead door, causing the airbags to deploy and the rear of the car to be completely squashed. The damage on the Lexus went from $5,000 to $18,000 just like that.

Then there was a Lincoln one of the Chasers brought into to shop. It had some minor front-end damage, nothing too crazy. A small job for the guys. But there was another Lincoln, same color and model, that had been hit in the rear end. Well, here was an opportunity to get a little extra money out of the job. The guys took the smashed-up parts off the one car and swapped it with the parts of the client's car to get the insurance company to pay extra for the damages. Then, after the insurance company cut the check, they'd just reinstall the original parts and fix the car up for the client. We made an extra $6,000, washed the Lincoln up, and returned the car to the client. All's well that ends well. Right?

I can't tell you how many times we smashed cars with little damages to make bigger ones just for the money. We would get good use out of the pole outside of the shop, and I can't remember how many times we'd have to replace the pole! That thing would get knocked out over and over again. We were making the money by any means necessary. And, when I say by any means, I mean by ANY means.

Water damage was a huge seller for us! Salt-water damage totals a car because of the metal rotting from the inside out. So, whenever there were news reports of storms and flooding in the shore areas like Atlantic City, Margate, Ocean City, etc.; it was like Christmas morning for us. But not how you might think. See, we kept bags of sand and seaweed at the shop. So, every scammer in Philly would come to the shop and drop of their car. They'd claim their car was towed (after we provided them with fake towing bills); and the guys would pour sand and seaweed all over the motor compartment, carpet floors, and seats. The clients who wanted to get rid of their cars would call their insurance companies; we'd label it a total loss and charge $3,000 for each car. Others who just needed a little extra cash, they'd split the check for repairs with the shop. Then, after the insurance adjuster left, we detailed the car and deliver it back to the client. We would just vacuum the sand out, wash off the seaweed, and clean the entire vehicle. No damage. It was an easy way to make a quick $5,000 - $10,000.

Everything was an opportunity to make more money. Unfortunately, for Moe's and Joey's business affairs, it wasn't enough. He had shifted his attention to the construction company, and I could already see where this was going. I loved that but I was always looking out for what was best for me and my family.

Chapter 6 – Chasing Green

I, finally, decided to meet with the owner of the shop in Northeast Philly, it was at their auto body shop, Luka's Auto Body & Repair. The place was only about a quarter the size of Moe's Collision and barely got any auto body work. In the whole 2 hours I was there, I only saw three trucks pull into the garage. The owner was a tall and bulky Russian man, nice guy but I could tell he was a "no nonsense" businessman. I looked around at the shop and the equipment, then he took me upstairs to his office. As I sat across from his desk and pressed through understanding his heavy accent, I got the sense there was a problem with his business, and he needed help, at any cost.

"My son, Jacob…he runs the shop. We have a mechanic shop two blocks away. This area…a lot of Russians here. The mechanic shop does very well. But the body shop, Jacob needs help." He grabbed his drink off his desk in utter disappointment. "Soon, we will be out of business." There was about 3 long minutes of silence between us as I thought about my response. "Mr. Pavlov," I replied, "I'm an extremely competitive person. I've been in the auto body business a long time, I'm up for the challenge and I know I can turn your shop around."

Now, I know what you're thinking. Why would anyone go from one of the largest shops in the city, a well-established business that had body work, day and night, and brought in half a million dollars to a dying shop a quarter of the size? Well, here's why; in our agreement, Mr. Pavlov increased my salary and I was now making $2000 more a month. He also promised I could have whatever car I wanted after the shop started making money. Plus, the size of the shop itself promised to be less stressful. Right now, with everything going on with Joey Mal, his side business, and the risks he was taking; less stress was exactly what I needed.

Now, I had earned quite a favorable reputation with the Chasers. I took care of them and they knew I was always going to get them the most money out of every job they brought to the shop. They also knew that I knew my numbers; I'd never let a shop owner lie about estimate totals; they liked that about me. So, when news hit that I was leaving Moe's Collision, it was no surprise they all followed me to Luka's. The small shop was overflowing with work in no time. The Chasers ended up loving the shop because we had two Mexican brothers named Vicente and Romano. They were nicknamed the "Mexicans," and for a bottle of Jose Cuervo, they would gladly add thousands of dollars of enhanced damage to any vehicle. The Chasers would come and request them all the time.

Then, one of the Chasers, Junior, hooked me up with, Steve Nichols, a Jersey lawyer who was taking all the limited tort cases in Philly. Back then, lawyers wouldn't touch limited tort. Full tort cases allowed them to sue for the maximum on a policy's limit; to them, there just wasn't enough money in limited tort cases to be worth working them. But for Steve, none of that mattered. If anything, it was an opportunity, and it was my opportunity to become a starting player in the game. Here was a chance to cash in from limited tort customers, and there was no way I was passing it up. Up until then, I had a minor role in the car crash ring; inflating estimates; but all that would soon change!

Steve had a small firm in South Jersey, but he had his license to practice in PA. Since the Chasers had come to me about these limited tort clients, I went to Steve. Soon, he was taking every limited tort case he could get. I was getting paid; the Chasers were getting paid. A whole new market had opened up and the shop was booming with jobs. Steve called me up, one day, and started talking to me about his doctor friend. He said his name was Mark Winston and he had two offices, one in Jersey and one in Philly. Dr. Winston was a close friend and, apparently, one night over dinner, they had been discussing his limited tort cases and how he was getting so many. Now, the doctor wanted in; and he was willing to pay $600 for every person I brought to him. Well, it didn't take long to fill the shop, the lawyer's office, the doctor's office, and my pockets.

Now, listen. As a shop manager, I made good money. Legitimately, I was making $4,000 a week. That should have been enough to make a decent life for my wife and kids. But I was in so deep, I was busy chasing green. I had a $3200 monthly mortgage payment; an electric bill that was $1200 a month in the summer and $800 in the winter; my kids were going to private school; and I was paying for my wife to attend law school. So, as far as I could see, I was hustling for them, for us. With everything I was doing, I was making $40,000 to $50,000 a month; and stashing it all away in my closet. No one knew, not even my wife. And, I intended to keep it that way. But, sooner or later, we all have to accept consequences.

Chapter 7 – The Major "Players"

Lawyers

Lawyer Steve got a lot of our business. As I mentioned, he was my point of contact anytime we would need to refer a client. But he wasn't the only lawyer in the mix. Many lawyers, in South Jersey and Philly, would pay (and some still do) for these clients they called the "accident ambulance chasers". When we were doing these enhanced damages and staging accidents, the lawyers were paying anywhere from $600 to $2500 a person, depending on their insurance coverage and whether they had full tort or limited tort on their insurance policies.

These lawyers were making big money, especially the large firm lawyers. They would catch 20 to 30 cases, and when you're getting 33% of each settlement; well that adds up. Let's just do the math on that. If a lawyer got 20 cases and, to make it easy, let's just say the settlement on each was $15,000 (of course, most times it was much more); then they're making $4,950 per case! That's almost $100,000. That's a pretty good payday. So, naturally, these law firms gave their clients whatever they asked for, Mercedes and tow trucks, anything!

The law firms didn't care. They knew these lavish gifts and the referral fees were nothing compared to the money they would get for each case they settled. Every day, these law firms would settle up to three cases. Some still solicit cases like these today. They continue to do this type of business and go on living their lives. And, somehow, this is considered legal?!

Doctors

It was amazing how much these "professionals" would pay to get the business. For us, it was easy money, so we kept pressing clients to sign up and meet with these lawyers and doctors, like Dr. Winston who was always top choice for me. But there was another doctor I'd work with just as often. Dr. Paul was a chiropractor who was paying $1500 per person, at that time. When the accidents involved multiple people, we'd make sure they went to his office as soon as we dropped the car off at the shop. Getting people to sign up wasn't exactly a hard sell either, since his office was next to the law firm.

In addition to the money, there were many perks to getting our clients over to the chiropractor. I've gotten tickets to see the Eagles, 76's, and the Flyers. I'd get the best seats money could buy – for free! Every Friday, I'd meet with the doctors and lawyers at the famous "Turf Club".

The problem with greed is that you can never have enough. Greed is insatiable. And, that's exactly what happened to one of the other chiropractor's we'd work with. He was getting slammed with business. His waiting room was insanely packed week after week. Eventually, a person didn't even have to go to get therapy. They'd show up and sign in, then leave. And, he'd bill their insurance company for all different types of therapy and procedures that they "supposedly" received, but he never did any of it. All he needed was a signature and he'd get paid; no need to waste your time waiting around – and most people were faking it for the lawsuit anyway!

Well, someone snitched, and the FBI caught wind of it. They sent an undercover federal agent into his office to sign up for therapy, claiming to have been in an accident. After a few visits, this agent tells the doctor that they can't miss work, but he could just bill the insurance company as if they'd been in his office. He told the doctor to just mark him down as present for therapy. This doctor was already signing others in for excessive therapy sessions and billing insurance companies, so he agreed. He had been doing it so long, he just couldn't stop. After a while and having a large number of insurance bills came through, the FBI had enough proof. They raided his office, took his patient records and all his files, closed the business, and locked the doctor up. They charged him on multiple counts of fraud. Needless to say, he lost his license along with four properties.

There was a medical doctor a few blocks from the chiropractor who, coincidentally, suffered the same fate. But he was able to write drug prescriptions. Back then, you could go back as many times as you wanted to get your prescription from doctors. So, it was no surprise, that this doctor would have lines wrapping around his office building. He would fill their prescriptions, but bill insurance company for medicine he never gave. Soon, people were getting hooked on Oxycodone & Percocet. This doctor contributed to the deaths of many. We all sin, greed can overtake any one of us, but this guy had taken it too far. Naturally, he lost his license and was sentences to jail.

I'm glad to say, I never referred anyone to this doctor; but even today there are "professionals" who abuse their right to practice for monetary gain. And, there are still people who look for these types of "services", to get money or drugs, falsified medical documents, etc. Whether it was a car accident or a "slip & fall", people show up to court with false claims, winning lawsuits and taking advantage of an imperfect system.

As you can see, things were getting shadier by the car crash! But I stayed in the game. I had even heard of one case in which an insurance company had hired a doctor and paid him well to evaluate a client's injury. He lied and was rewarded handsomely for reporting that they weren't injured so the insurance company wouldn't have to pay their treatment anymore. On the flip side, he also had his own practice in which he'd bill insurance companies for extra treatments for clients who didn't need it. Incredible.

Insurance Adjusters

I've worked at shops in both Jersey and Philadelphia, and I can tell you one major difference is that Philly has a lot more Damage Appraisers than Jersey does. And, like everything else in the "big city", it wasn't hard to find adjusters who would inflate your vehicle damage cost if you made it worth their while. For a few hundred dollars, they had no problem doctoring their reports. It was easy to get a car with $4,000 worth of damage be listed as $10,000 in damages on their reports. Yes, we'd get the insurance company to pay an extra $6,000.

These adjusters were experienced, and they knew what they were doing. They knew exactly what to write and what to add on that would increase the value of the car damage. They could make anywhere from $1000, to $4,000 a day by inflating damage reports. They even knew which shops would pay them to do these types of things. Yeah, they worked for the insurance companies, but they didn't care. To them, it was all about the money.

On several occasions, I witnessed these payoffs between shop owners and adjusters. They both reaped a harvest from inflated car damages. One lady, an insurance adjuster, not only falsified her report, but she actually grabbed a hammer and added more damage to the car herself so she could increase the estimate. I'll never forget it. My face must've sold me out because she looked at me and admitted that she didn't care about her insurance company. She said she needed to pay her bills. Hey, I guess she felt she had to handle business.

All these so-called professionals were major players in this large insurance fraud ring. It was one big cycle we had collectively created. And, for a while, it seemed like (with the exception of a few hiccups) it was all working well, and everyone was getting rich and living well. But things were about to go south. It started with a series of little events that, when added up, would create a heck of a lot of chaos and turn everyone's life upside down.

Chapter 8 – Gone Sideways

Jacob came to the shop one day to see how everything was going. He and his dad were pleased with how well the shop was doing. Everything was great, until he told me about his friend. A Chaser named Pauly. Pauly had asked Jacob for one of our tow trucks, promising to bring all kinds of work into the shop. The shop was already exceeding, but Jacob knew the guy from years ago. He had worked for the Russians before and Jacob swore Pauly was good on his word. Since he knew Pauly and trusted Jacob, I thought, 'Why not, the more the better.' But, little did I know, this would be the start of a disastrous finish to the dealings with Chasers, lawyers, and doctors.

Pauly made good on his word alright. He brought more work to the shop, just not how I thought. He had people buying new cars from car dealerships, then after a few months, he'd smash them up and tow them to Luka's. His friend, a police officer named Danny, would write false police reports on the incidents for $500 each. He'd put people's names on the reports, claiming they were in the vehicles when they were nowhere near the accident.

This Chaser was smashing everything from Cadillacs to Mercedes; all brand new. The estimates on these cars were ridiculously high, and the higher the estimate the higher the commission. And, with Danny's help,

Pauly was bringing 8-10 people a week to my lawyer and doctor contacts. My regular weekly salary was peanuts compared to what I was making on this side hustle.

Other Chasers wanted in on some action, too. It was my idea, but they convinced shop employees to jack up the back of their tow trucks and place a 4x4 piece of wood under it to make it look like the whole tow truck bed was twisted. Then they'd call the insurance company and say they had been hit from behind. So, I'd write up a $30,000 estimate for them. I have to say this was genius; the average insurance adjuster in Philadelphia couldn't even write up a regular car properly, let alone the equipment on a tow truck. And, they didn't have any pricing on tow truck parts in their database, so they had no choice but to take my estimates. After I went over the tow truck "damage" with them, they'd hand the driver a check for $20,000, sometimes more. When they left, we'd remove the piece of wood from under the truck, tighten everything back up, and the driver would speed off with their money. There was never even a scratch on their truck. I would get $9,000 to $10,000 for being the brains of this idea.

You might be asking how the adjusters would so blindly rely on my estimates. Well, since they didn't have pricing on parts, I did all the research for them. I would call the truck manufacturers and get directed to the parts department. Then, I'd ask them for pictures and prices for the parts; I put everything in a folder for the adjuster. What would've taken them days to figure out, I did in a matter of minutes. This made them look good because they had all the research they needed. I can't tell you how many times we pulled this off, but it worked, and everyone was making money.

Then, Pauly starts hooking up with this girl, Marla, who he had met at one of the nightclubs in Center City. Little petite, young thing with long jet-black hair. She was a city native from a very wealthy family. Not sure what she was doing with a guy like Pauly, but my guess was she was one of those rebellious rich-girl types. Pauly, as usual, had lied to her mom and told her he owned an auto body shop. Now, Pauly had a real smooth lip, and he had talked Marla's mom into buying 5 cars, 3 new ones from a dealership in Mayfair and 2 used cars from a place further down. He walked into the shop and talked to Jacob about these vehicles. Now, I don't typically listen in on conversations, but I didn't trust Pauly as far as I could throw him. So, as I'm listening, I hear him say, "Jacob, you know I'm good for it. Just give me $15,000. I'll bring you 4 out of the 5 cars next week, and you can do whatever you need to. Damage them any way you want. This is a good deal."

Something in my gut just didn't sit well with what Pauly was saying, but Jacob agreed and wrote out a $15,000 check. Maybe it was the fact that Pauly was shady or maybe that his girlfriend was standing right there and was, obviously, caught up on the whole fraud ring. I just don't know, but in the moment, I knew the whole thing was going sideways. Either way, it was done; and Pauly and Marla took the check and headed straight for the check-cashing place down the street. Jacob got the 4 cars and backed them into the frame machine causing about $10,000 more in damages per car. He got his money and more, I couldn't help but to think at what cost.

And, my gut wasn't wrong. Later I found out the FBI got the security tape from the check cashing place to prove it was all fraud. They went to Marla, who was the easiest target, and threatened her with federal charges. So, she told them everything she knew, soup to nuts, just to get herself out of trouble with the FBI and the District Attorney's office.

Chapter 9 – The Hook Up

Pauly was a complete pain in my backside, but there was one thing that kept him around – he was the "hook up." He had an "in" with a guy named Casey, he was the manager of a new car dealership not too far from the shop. Because of Pauly's friendship with Casey, he was getting people with no or bad credit approved for brand new cars. And, it wasn't even like it took any time. Casey was handing out same day approvals like it was Black Friday.

The only problem was that, after two months, these people couldn't afford the monthly car payments anymore. Truthfully, we all know they shouldn't have gotten these cars in the first place, but who was I to judge. So, Pauly starts helping these people stage accidents and damage their cars. Then, he'd tow the cars to the shop, get paid the commission for the damages, and give people the money they needed. Some of these cars would come in the shop 2 or 3 times a year. This was how they managed to keep their cars and pay them month by month.

I'm estimating here, but if Pauly brought 100 people to the dealership to get a new car, at least 50% of them would wind up in the same financial bind. They weren't able to make those payments, but this was an opportunity for Pauly to make extra cash, and (I guess) "help" them, too. Believe it or not, he wasn't the only chaser who started doing this. There's another one who STILL brings people to this dealership. And, Casey is still there pre-approving people who have no business buying new cars. And, not just any cars; these were high-end luxury vehicles.

We're talking Mercedes, BMW, Land Rovers; just to name a few. This worked well for the chasers because the more expensive the car, the more value in damages. Casey didn't mind, of course. His job was to get sales, and that' what he did. His sales were skyrocketing which meant higher commission for him too. The how didn't matter, just the what. Now, Pauly and this other chaser were the only ones I knew of pulling this scheme. But there might have been others.

Sly was another chaser who had ALL the hook-ups. He was a true hustler, all the way around. He lived out of his truck and stayed out day and night waiting for accidents. He had lawyers and doctors in his pocket, and he'd let them know the terms of their relationship without hesitation. He brought them so many clients, one doctor bought him a Mercedes, 2-door convertible. As if that wasn't enough, the law firm - they bought him his own customized tow truck. These people knew that for the amount of work he'd bring them weekly, it was worth spending the money on him to keep him happy.

Because of all the business he got them, the medical practice had a nice and spacious office with the most updated medical equipment and vans to pick their clients up from their homes and make sure they got treatment. Even the law firms in their big fancy office buildings on the 20th floor. Every dollar they got from insurance companies paid for their space, their fancy signs, their new cars, vacation homes, sporting event tickets (which most of the time, they'd give away) – all of it was thanks to the chasers, especially Sly.

Not all chasers conducted business like this – staging accidents and getting freebies. In fact, I liked working with the "old school" chasers better because they had a conscience and treated accident chasing like a job, not a scam. There are respectable and honest chasers, even now. There are guys who aren't willing to sell their souls for money.

Chapter 10 – The Chaser's Life

Some people might think these events are crazy, stupid, and irresponsible. But, in my line of work and back in those days, it was just another day in the life of a Chaser. These guys needed their money, and they did whatever it took to get it. Eventually, the insurance hustle had morphed into all different kinds of fraud. It wasn't just waiting on accidents and lying about tow truck damage. Now, staging accidents and people became a thing and, somehow, I still couldn't see the downward spiral, but it was coming. You wouldn't believe the stories I heard and lived with some of these Chasers. The accident business was lucrative, but somehow, it was never enough. And, these next two stories should have been a sign to get out. Too bad I had missed it.

The Story of Two Chasers

Worm-man (that was his nickname, of course) was one of the best Chasers at our shop. I never knew why they called him that, I only assumed it was because he was really tall, white, and thin. He looked like a stick of uncooked spaghetti. But he would always bring us work, all different hours. Sometimes, I wondered if the guy ever slept. One day, Worm-man rents a car and goes to pick up his friend, Richie, who had just gotten out of jail. Richie needed money fast, so Worm-man thought it was a good idea to pay Richie $500 to ram Richie's car into the rental on I-95 South in rush hour traffic.

At the time, I was also in the car along with Worm-man's neighbors, Pete and Arty. After the first time Richie drove into the rental, Worm-man got another bright idea. He had the worst teeth I'd ever seen this side of the Ben Franklin, so he thought we should jam the car again, but this time with a string attached to a few of his teeth. Since I was in the back seat, I told him to hand me the string and I'd pull them. Richie rammed the car into Worm-man's car once more, and this time, I yanked four of Worm-man's teeth; they came flying out and hit the back window. Worm-man screamed, and blood was everywhere. Then a man in a black Toyota Camry pulled over on the shoulder of the highway and headed towards our car. I told Worm-man to spit the blood all over the dash and window; when the man came up to the driver's side, he grabbed a radio and called in the ambulance. Turned out he was an off-duty cop. Just our luck, we were taken to all different hospitals, and the next day we were all at the lawyer and doctor's office. Naturally, Worm-man got brand new teeth out of this shenanigan. Matter of fact, he got brand new teeth and a $75,000 lawsuit. And, when he told the FBI and District Attorney about the whole set-up, he got a free ride out just for ratting us out. He earned his nickname; he was a real worm.

But, if you thought that was crazy, wait until you hear the next one. There was nothing these Chasers wouldn't do for money, and most were decent guys, but there were some I just didn't mess with. One of those was a grease ball named Guido. I avoided him like a plague. Guido and his friend Marco never came around unless they needed something, and usually it cost the shop employees more grief than anything else. These two were the brokest jokers in the world, and I knew that's why they came to me with their dumb stuff.

Guido and Marco called me about this incident with Guido's year-old silver Mercedes. He spent his entire lawsuit money on it and had blown the motor. So, he asks me for a solution. Where was I supposed to get a new motor for his Mercedes? He didn't even have money for a tow! So, I called my Chaser buddy, Willy and asked him for a favor. Willy and his nephew, Chad, went to Jersey to pick up the car, Guido, and Marco; and brought them back to Philly. They stopped at one of the dark alley streets a few blocks from Luka's and Guido and Marco got back in the Mercedes. Once they were in, Chad rammed into the Mercedes a few times causing about $15,000 in damages. Guido called the cops, the cops called an ambulance for him & Marco, then Willy brought the car to the shop.

All of this for a new motor. Well, Willy got his cut of 20% for the tow and gave Chad his share. Guido and Marco got 2 settlements from this staged accident. They both got about $80,000 in their lawsuits. Guido, of course, got his car back. After the repairs, that

Mercedes looked brand new with a new motor under the hood. I tell you, the things these yanksters did. And, you might think it was a slick deal, but this one would add fuel to the fire that was about to set off in our little ring. See, they might have seemed tough, but they completely cracked under pressure from the FBI. Looking back, I wish I'd never even answered the phone that day.

The Card Game Scheme

Rico and Jax were a couple of Chasers who usually brought work to Luka's. They were regulars, but they were also big gamblers, so they always needed money. One Friday morning in April, they came up with the most amazing plan; and it would've ended well had they thought it all through. See, in this business, the more people you involve the more money you get, but there's one problem with that. People are fickle, and the more you involve, the higher risk you take.

Rico came up with this story about planning a card game at his house in the Bustleton section of Northeast Philly. Jax, Rico's girlfriend Yahaira, and her younger sister Maria all met up at his place. Rico parked his 2006 navy blue Maxima right in front of his rowhome. Jax had brought his eagle-claw tow truck and parked it right behind the Maxima. Yahaira convinced her sister to rent a Dodge Caravan and pretend to slam into the tow truck which would then cause the tow truck to slam into Rico's Maxima. Now, there was no real impact because they didn't want the cops sending anyone to the hospital. They just needed the report. So, when they called the cops, they made sure to place a two by four under the tow truck to make it look damaged. Since the cop had taken about an hour to get to the scene and had no clue how much damage was done to the cars, he just took everyone's statements and left.

The next day, Rico and Jax brought the Maxima to Luka's and had Jacob enhance the rear-end damage to the Maxima by backing it into the frame machine. Now, there was about $9000 worth of damage to it, and $32,000 worth for the "supposed" tow truck rear damage; totaling $33,000! Rico's "card game" also resulted in $6,600 in commission, $6,000 to Jacob for using the shop, I got paid for writing up the estimate, and Rico only paid $2000 to get the car repaired. Not a bad game of cards, if I do say so myself.

Unfortunately, I wasn't saying so myself! Remember Yahaira and her sister Maria? Well, what the Chasers didn't know was that Maria was pregnant and had a lot more to lose than Rico and Jax. While we were living life, the FBI was now conducting an ongoing investigation on automobile insurance fraud. Now, I don't know how, but they got in contact with Maria and she agreed to cooperate with them. She told them all about Rico's genius card game scheme. To make matters worse, when they reached out to him, he said nothing. Instead, he went to Maria's house and threatened to beat her. So, she went back to the FBI and they locked him up. Now, even though I had nothing to do with their scheme, when Maria & Yahaira were questioned, my name was mentioned, and charges were brought on me right along with the Chasers.

After that, they found Jax who was a coward and decided to blurb my name to the FBI like I had anything to do with their plan. But I didn't even know what these jerks had done until they brought the Maxima and tow truck to the shop. They were acting like it was my idea, and I knew they had cut a deal to get me caught. I know I had done a lot of bad stuff, but there was no way I was going down for something I didn't do. Rico and Jax had each called me on separate occasions, asking for money for lawyers, and trying to get me to admit I was in on it. I knew the call was being recorded and, like I said, I wasn't going to fess up to something that had nothing to do with me. As far as I was concerned, they had no tangible proof against me, and I was clean as a whistle.

A few days after that, Guido called me (again) about an Audi A-8. He was having a hard time selling it and wanted to have it smashed and totaled. Of course, I hook him up with Big Dave. Big Dave was a 6 foot 5, 450-pound black man who was always about his business. He came around every now and then but was careful not to get too close to the other Chasers. In hindsight, now I know why. Anyway, Big Dave struck a deal with Guido and charged him $1500 for the wreck. He took the keys and smashed the car up until it was totaled. All good, but there was one problem and the problem's name was Marla (yes, again). In the midst of all their planning, Pauly had asked Big Dave to put his girl Marla in the car. He, then, got a falsified police report and went to see our lawyer buddy, Steve, and the good old doctor. All three got a big payday. But Marla (who we already knew was nothing but trouble) was another one that ended up in the mix. She was questioned and it didn't take much to get her to talk. Shocker.

About two week later, Worm-man called me on my cell phone. Of all people! Something was up. He started saying the same things Jax and Rico had said before. The FBI and Northeast detectives had gotten to him, too. Now, he was trying to set me up. He was putting out the bait, but I wasn't biting. I knew what was going on. One by one, they were going down; and they wanted to take me down with them.

Chapter 11 – "Greed-Eyed" Monster

Even while all this is going on with the FBI's investigation, I thought there was no way they had anything on me. As far as I was concerned, I was squeaky clean, and it was now time to cash in on a promise. Luka's was doing very well, getting work in from Chasers all over the area. So, I decided to meet with Jacob about his dad's promise to give me the vehicle of my choice. The shop had turned around, it was making more than enough money. I had held up my end and now it was time for them to hold up theirs.

You should've seen old man Pavlov's face when Jacob told him to go to the dealership and sign for my brand new jet-black 4 door Mercedes-Benz S550 with cream color leather interior. I didn't speak a lick of Russian, but from what I could tell the old man was not happy. He still signed, though; let's be honest, he was going to shut Luka's down had it not been for me. And, deep down, he knew the Chasers would follow me anywhere.

It was life as usual, until Jacob decided to bring his brand-new Chevy Conversion Van to the shop. He had a few of the guys strip the interior completely. I'm talking passenger seats, entertainment system, down to the airbags. Then, he drove back to his house, removed the driver's seat, called the cops to report the car stolen and left the car at a school parking lot 3 miles down. And, he might have gotten away with it, if his car wasn't armed with a very well-known, built-in GPS and tracking system. That dummy. They were able to track every location of the vehicle, so they knew it hadn't been stolen at all. They arrested Jacob, and that left me at the shop until he got out.

This wasn't exactly a good thing, considering one of the Stefano brothers from Stefano Towing Company started bringing work from West Philly. They had heard about the 20% commission at Luka's from another Chaser. Time had passed and Jacob was back at the shop. After a few months of dealing with these guys, they were bringing so many cars, it was tough for Pavlov and Jacob to keep up with the weekly commission checks. They couldn't give advances anymore, instead they'd wait for the insurance payments to come through before paying out commission.

Heavy D, the oldest of the Stefano brothers was not one to wait for his money. So, one day, he tows 5 cars into the garage and tells old man Pavlov that they already had estimates done and he wanted to get paid on the spot or he'd take the cars to some other shop. He pressured Pavlov into writing him a $12,000 check based on those estimates. Then, he took the check and disappeared. Well, it turns out, those estimates were all fake. Heavy D had gotten his friend to write them up. Then, he sneaked back in later that night and took the cars to another shop and got paid with legitimate estimates over there. He was a complete sleaze ball and, that day, the Russians learned a very valuable lesson – never play with Chasers' money. They got double-crossed and couldn't do anything about it! Chasers didn't let anyone mess with their cash, and if you did, it would not fair you well.

A few weeks later, Guido was back. I told you this guy only showed up when he needed something. So, imagine my surprise when he came into the shop asking me for help, once again. This time, he needed a favor with another Audi, but it was his own car. Apparently, Big Dave wasn't around. But I wasn't having it either. I had enough dealing with his Mercedes' motor fiasco. Heavy D happened to be at the shop talking to one of my guys, so I took advantage of the opportunity to get Guido off my back. I introduced him to Heavy D, I thought 'The sleaze ball and the grease ball, a slimy match made in heaven.' They talked for a while, then Guido thanked me and left.

Next day, Guido calls me asking for the phone numbers of the doctor and the lawyer I was working with. He said his friend Lugo had paid Heavy D $1400 to smash his Audi to the point of total loss. Guido wanted the car to be totaled so he could collect all the insurance money. Our good old friend Danny the cop had written up a fake report for Heavy D. The only catch was that Heavy D wanted his girlfriend Tanesha to be placed at the scene too, in the car with Guido and Lugo. What is it with these people and their girlfriends? Imagine, two white guys from Jersey in an Audi with a black girl from North Philly. That right there was always one of Heavy D's problems, he was always chasing the "greed-eyed monster," never turning down an opportunity to make a dollar.

Heavy D's other problem? His girl, Tanesha. That girl was crazy and Heavy D had a bad temper. They always fought about everything, and D would beat her senseless. But she was always coming back! After he would stage his accidents with her, sometimes he'd take all the money for himself and give her nothing. So, I guess she had enough and went to the FBI. Hell hath no fury like a woman scorned! D found out what she had done, he took her mother's black Mercedes-Benz 380L 2-seater and painted it gold; then, he went into hiding.

If these Chasers were crazy, their girls were crazier. I had never met more jacked up women in my life. They didn't care as long as it was benefiting their own. And, none were crazier than this girl, Tanesha. The things she did just to spite Heavy D were unbelievable! They were constantly at each other's throats. I didn't get that relationship. But I'll tell you what, we all paid the price for her crazy. When she got picked up by the FBI for this scam, we were all thrown under the bus, one by one.

Chapter 12 – Trouble at the Shop

The FBI and the detectives from the Philadelphia District Attorney's office were working together to build a bullet proof case against us. They already had statements from Yahaira and her pregnant sister, then Jacob's stolen Chevy disaster put an even bigger spotlight on the shop, and now, they had Tanesha spilling out her guts! Remember Marla, Pauly's girl? Somehow, they'd gotten to her, too. I knew that one was coming back to bite us. Everything was starting to come together for the feds like pieces of a really jacked up puzzle! And, every piece pointed back to one place – Luka's Auto Body & Repair.

So, not only were these girls cutting deals with the feds, but Rico, Jax, and Worm-man did, too. We didn't know who to trust, so we had to make sure we were extra careful at the shop. Now, our only saving grace was that the detectives still didn't have hard evidence against the shop. All they had were sworn statements from grimy people trying to cut the best deal they could with the FBI.

The detectives started paying us frequent visits, trying to intimidate the guys at the shop and put all the information they had together. But we just kept our cool and acted like we knew nothing every time. We all knew, when the detectives were around, the shop was like Fort Knox. No one had been indicted yet, so it was business as usual for us.

In the plaza where the shop was there was also a Russian mechanic shop. The owner, Gustav, had a 2003 Mercedes he wanted to get rid of, so he came to me for help. Of course, the first person I thought of for the job was Heavy D. So, I got him on the phone with Gustav, and they made a pretty sweet deal. For $500, Heavy D agreed to take Gustav's Mercedes down by the river and set the car on fire. It burned down to the springs in the seats. And, later that week, Gustav was driving a brand-new charcoal-gray Lexus SUV. Who would've known Gustav would turn out to be another yankster like the rest of them? There was just no telling who you could trust, now.

From Bad to Worse

Jacob had a mother-in-law named Selma who was highly addicted to prescription pills. Every week, this lady would figure out a way to get pills from the neighborhood pharmacy. After Jacob got out of jail from his little "stolen" van incident, he purchased a 2005 Lincoln LS. Months go by, and he decides he's tired of the Lincoln. So, he takes Selma for a ride on Route 95 North. About 15 minutes into the ride, he takes the Lincoln and runs it straight into the wall just off the ramp of one of the exits.

Jacob called one of the Chasers to have the car towed into the shop. The damage came out to about $13,000 worth, but that wasn't good enough. Jacob needed money and Selma needed pills. So, he had the

Mexicans run the Lincoln into the frame machine, then turn and back it into the machine again. There was extensive damage to the front and rear. When I wrote the estimate again, the damages went from $13,000 to $22,000. As soon as the insurance money cut the check, Jacob disappeared; him and his mother-in-law.

His car, on the other hand, sat there on the frame machine for over a month and a half. Jacob had blown through the money and couldn't afford to purchase the parts for the repair. Things at the shop were going from bad to worse. All the money they were getting in didn't matter a lick. No matter how much I'd give Pavlov and his son to deposit on Fridays, by Monday morning it was gone. Every Monday, without fail, they'd come to me and tell me they didn't have enough for payroll. And, then, expected me to come up with a solution. Every week, I was sweating bullets trying to call customers and convince them to use their insurance checks and save on deductibles. I'd even drive a few of them to their insurance agency office to pick up their checks. For six years, I did whatever it took to make sure everyone got paid. To this day, I don't understand what those Russians did with the money. I might have expected it from Jacob, but I don't know when old man Pavlov changed. They had money for new tow trucks, new machines, and new cars; but never for payroll. It was crazy.

Then Jacob started showing up at the shop less. He would come in Monday and Tuesday, then disappear the rest of the week. Week after week, he kept showing up one or two days until he just stopped showing up altogether. He had a monitor at his house that allowed him to see the shop through the cameras they had installed. Instead of coming into the shop, he'd just watch the guys work from the comfort of his own home. One time, he met me at Luka's around 5:30 in the morning (before anyone else got there) to discuss some things he had seen through the cameras. I, later, found out Jacob was hooked on prescription pills too.

When old man Pavlov found out what his son was doing, he was hot. He asked me to go talk to Jacob, but what difference was that going to make? My job was to run the shop, make sure everyone got paid, and the Chasers got their commission. That's exactly what I did. I couldn't stop Jacob from popping pills. And, he was only getting worse. When his doctor stopped prescribing them to him, he'd pay his friends anywhere from $60 to $80 for pills. It was all downhill from there.

Chapter 13 – More Money, More Problems

A few weeks later, Jacob calls me up and says Heavy D was going to pick up three of our tow trucks. He didn't say why, but I figured something crooked was about to go down. When D showed up, he told me Jacob had called him because he needed more money. So, he asked Heavy D to get rid of our three oldest trucks. It made sense because Jacob couldn't sell them. Those trucks were so worn from Chasers hauling vehicles day and night, no one was going to pay for them. The only way he was getting any money out of those trucks was by totaling them and collecting all the insurance money, and that was Heavy D's specialty.

Heavy D almost never worked alone. So, on this job, he recruited two other Chasers named Otto and Fat Fred. They took the trucks and crashed into one another causing thousands worth of damage. But Jacob's grand scheme almost didn't work because when the "heavy equipment certified" insurance adjuster came he wrote out only $11,000 in damages for one of the trucks. So, I had the Mexicans put the truck on the lift and walked the adjuster through every damaged part on the truck. His boss called me, asking questions about the truck, and then came out to the shop to see for himself. He couldn't believe all the damage that was done and how his guy missed it. They had no choice but to total the tow truck and cut a check for $21,000. D, Fat Fred, and Otto split the commission; they each got about $4,000 on that one. It was astronomical the amount of money those insurance companies paid out to Luka's, and no one ever bothered to question it.

In fact, a lot of the adjusters in Philly were more than happy to take bribes for accepting bogus estimates. Nothing like the insurance adjusters in Jersey; it was a whole different world over the bridge. Depending on the vehicle, I could write a $10,000 estimate from a $1,500 job. The adjuster would get $1,500 for taking the estimate, and all is well that ends well. (Mostly).

The thing is, that old saying "with more money comes more problems," was literally the shop's mantra. Shop employees would bring in money, I'd bring in money, and who knows what Pavlov and his son would do with it. Once, one of my guys took parts from a customer's Chevy Blazer to fix another customer's Chevy and bring in a quick $9,000. Then he called the other client and asked him to bring the insurance check so he could buy his parts, the client agreed so long as we saved them the $500 deductible. The customer brought the check in to the shop, but Jacob never used it to purchase his parts. This happened with client after client; every week, and it was like the Russians thought the money was just falling from the sky. They spent it on everything except what it was supposed to be used for! It wasn't long before customers started blowing up our phone wondering why their cars weren't ready. But we didn't have the parts to make the repairs because there was no money.

Everyone was just about their getting their own and the customers were paying for it. One of the adjusters, who was known for taking bribes, wrote out a $9,000 estimate and, instead of mailing the check to the client like he was supposed to, he took his $1500 cut and left the check on the counter. So, here I had another client with no parts for his car and no money to get it repaired. The way Pavlov and Jacob were acting, I knew it wouldn't be long before they closed shop for good. I don't even think they had bank accounts. Every check they got went straight to the check cashier's and everyone was always paid in cash.

Eventually, customers got tired of hearing the lame excuses. They got tired of hearing that their car parts were on back order or that the shop was extremely busy and that we had to push back repair time. And, I didn't blame them either. I was as good with my customers as I was with my estimates. I believed in giving quality work and I always made sure they got their repairs done in a decent amount of time. At least, that's how it was the first few years at Luka's. But the money made that all change. The customers were now reporting the shop and the detectives caught wind of it. It was only a matter of time before the FBI was back in our hair. Meanwhile, old man Pavlov and his son seemed to be trying to stash all the money they could before going out of business and skipping out of town.

The customer complaints just kept piling and the detectives were putting the pressure on. Insurance companies couldn't help these people, I couldn't help these people. We all just started accepting the foreseen future that the shop would soon be closed, the money was gone, and these people's cars would be stuck in the lot. That's exactly how it went down. All the guys split, and I wound up back in Jersey at a small shop just outside of Runnemede.

Chapter 14 – The Heat was On

In those last six years, there were thousands of people making false claims and running to crooked doctors and lawyers, thousands of cars with inflated damages and estimates totaling $15,000; $20,000; and even $30,000! There were dirty cops writing hundreds of false accident reports. All to make a quick buck. Now, these complaints were giving the FBI a reason to track me down. They were looking to question me and find out what part I played in this mess.

The Chasers were only making matters worse. Even though they were the ones towing the cars to the shop, increasing the damages on the cars, and getting paid on those estimates; they were blaming everything on Pavlov, Jacob, and the shop. They were the ones smashing their own personal vehicles and tow trucks, but they thought nothing of that. It was all the shop's fault. It was Pavlov and Jacob. But as the shop's general manager, being thrown in the mix was inevitable. Especially since I was the one who had to answer for these unrepaired vehicles that were just sitting in the lot. I was the one who had to keep giving these people excuses and apologizing week after week. All I could say to the detectives was that I just worked there. I knew nothing and never got anything extra but my weekly pay.

But, by this time, the FBI was questioning everybody; and they arrested anyone they could, trying to put the case together. At first, I said nothing of course. I was sticking to my version as hard as I could. But the detectives kept coming around and putting pressure on everyone. Soon, they had those so-called tough guys singing like birds. The Chasers were telling everybody else's business just to save their own skin. Even the beloved Mexicans were dishing out information in exchange for immunity. People were selling out left and right, and the FBI detectives were making as many deals as possible. The heat was on and, when I sit back and think about it, none of it was worth all this.

The FBI had finally gotten a hold of Heavy D's whereabouts. They pulled him over on Roosevelt Blvd and, as they were walking over to his car, D sped off, hitting one of the agents. Needless to say, he was caught and charged with assaulting a federal agent on top of all his other charges. Heavy D was sentenced with 87 months in prison without parole. Since they had Heavy D in custody, it was only a matter of time before they got to our cop friend, Danny. Not only had he falsified police reports; but, on one occasion, he had his car smashed for money with D's help of course. I can only assume, that's how they were able to link them. To this day, Heavy D remains in jail. Danny, on the other hand, had made bail and decided to cooperate with the FBI. No telling what kind of additional dirt he had; the city was full of corruption.

Chapter 15 – When the "Players" Fold

There were some heavy hitters in this fraud ring. As you know, there was everything from chasers to doctors, to lawyers and police officers. That's right, Danny wasn't the only crooked cop. The ones who swore to protect and serve were protecting their wallets and serving their pockets. They all referred to each other and they all cashed in from it.

And, here's how it would work: if you were looking to score an accident with a certain number of people (because the more people the better the settlement), then the cop would falsify the report for a small fee of $500. They would write a legit police report, describing the accident and location, listing the amount of people you wanted, and documenting the injuries you wanted the report to state. Then, they'd sign the report as if they'd been to the scene of the accident. But, to be honest, most of the time, they weren't even there. They just took the money and wrote up whatever you wanted. I know it's unbelievable, but every bit of it is the God's honest truth! Hundreds of reports, never a real accident!

They All Came Crashing Down

Doctors, lawyers, Chasers, shop owners; everyone who was anyone was getting indicted. Over 240 people indicted in a five-year long investigation. One by one, each Chaser involved went crashing down and their only escape was to sell everyone else out. It was a whole mess of an investigation and the trial wasn't any better.

The FBI was able to track Jacob and Pavlov down. They were charged with 17 counts of insurance fraud and money laundering. They got a $300,000 fine and two years of jail time. Funny though, Worm-man, Rico, Jax and many others had suddenly vanished. Nothing was mentioned about them, they just walked away free. Remember Guido and Marco, and the whole Mercedes motor deal? Well, Guido was placed under house arrest and got a $100,000 fine. But Marco walked away untouched and actually *received* $50,000 from his lawsuit as a passenger in the Mercedes. 'Now, ain't that something,' I thought, 'involved in the plot but gets to walk away for talking. Unreal.'

Same thing happened with Marla, Pauly's girl. Remember how she and Pauly talked her rich mom into buying the 5 cars? Remember how she got $15,000 to split with him? Well, she walked away, no time and no fines. Crazy Tanesha, Heavy D's girl, who helped him with almost every staged accident he ever planned. She was another one that walked away unscathed. So many got away and they knew they were guilty, but they were clever enough to make deals with the District Attorney's office. Everything: the scams, the investigation, the trials; it was all coming to an end. But it was still my turn. I just wanted to be done with it all.

I was tired of it all. I mean, I've known of people throwing tarps over the roofs of their homes, dab the corners of their ceilings with coffee, and get new roofs out of it. Boat owners purposely leave their $400,000 boats in the water hoping for a big storm. And, when a storm comes, it causes anywhere from $50,000 to $100,000 worth of damage. I've seen people who frequent the shore, causing the salt-water to damage their car, call their insurance to declare it totaled after a flood storm. I've even heard of someone selling electronics that they knew were recalled because they caught on fire. They'd sell these electronics and the things would catch on fire and the businesses or buyers would collect on the property insurance. People slip and fall in stores, then sue the store for their own personal gain. "Slip and falls" happen almost every day! Let's face it, people scam insurance companies in different ways, every day. The only difference is that they don't get caught. I'm not saying it's right, and I'm not justifying what we did. But it happens, even today. Like I said, we just got caught.

Chapter 16 – My Day in Court

After being harassed for five years throughout their investigation and after all the phone calls I had received, it was finally my turn. It was my day in court and, if I can be honest, I just wanted it to be over. All of it. I was tired and stressed more than you can imagine. But there was unfinished business and I had to face the consequences. Before the court date, the DA's office took an assessment of all my income and assets. My salary during that time was $2,000 a week and our home was valued at $750,000. So, they added all our bills and then subtracted that number from the total assets.

In 2010, the day of sentencing came. Much to my surprise, my wife and her friend who worked for the prosecutor's office showed up in the court room. I wasn't sure what to expect, this entire situation had been rough on our family. Honestly, I thought this would be something I'd be facing alone, but her presence there was enough support. It gave me new perspective. What I had, without the money, was enough. I just never saw it.

I remember my stress level skyrocketing and my hands were sweaty. All these crazy thoughts of "would've, should've, could've" kept creeping in my head. All the things I would've done differently. But it was too late now. There was no going back. All I could do was sit in that court room, in the uncomfortable wooden chair and wait for the judge to tell me my fate. The judge looked up after what seemed like hours of silence and looked me straight in the face.

The judge sentenced me to 5 years of probation, 1500 hours of community service, and a $479,000 fine. $479,000?! They made me pay $100 a week for life! Considering I had heard about other people's sentencing and their fines, I was pissed. But as much as that sucked, I had to admit there was a lot to be grateful for. At the end of the day, I was involved in a pretty big way and it could've been a whole lot worse. I could've been locked up for ten years, that option was on the table at one point. If I have to pay $100 a week for the rest of my life in exchange for the ability to breathe fresh air, eat good food, and (most importantly) be with my family; I'll take it.

I can't deny what I did. I did it, took responsibility for it, and I'm paying my debt back. Was it all worth it? Not at all. But I can't afford to look back on the past. I can't change what was already done. What I can do is make sure my choices in the future are different. I can make sure I think things through. We all have the ability to get God-given wisdom, and that's what I go by now. I don't just move, not without His wisdom.

Chapter 17 – New Day, New Man

Two weeks before Christmas, my wife served me with divorce papers. I should've seen it coming, but I guess I just expected us to pull through. I thought we'd stick this one out, but I was wrong. I was hurt for a while, but it was time to move on. I needed to get my life back on track.

As I reflect on everything I lived through, I did what I had to do to give my family the best life I could. Yes, there's a lot I should've thought all the way through. I should've weighed the consequences. I made a lot of mistakes. We could've lived more modestly. I was caught up in keeping up with our lavish lifestyle, new cars, our $100,000 pool and deck, and fancy vacations. Now, I realize none of it mattered. None of that was worth all that I had to give up in return. If I could get a do-over, I would have never gotten involved. I lost my wife, my house, my dignity. After that, I couldn't get a job with any shops that dealt with insurance companies. The collision business was all I knew, it's what I was legitimately good at. I was basically starting over at 55 years old.

My whole life has been tough, and I learned a lot of things at a very young age. But, if there's one thing I know for sure it's that everyone makes mistakes and after a fight, you have to get back up, brush the dirt off your shoulders, and keep it moving. I've been fighting all my life, and I wasn't going to quit now. I went back to church and started putting God first in everything I did. I found a great church in Westville, Victory in Christ Christian Center, that actually teaches how to live life according to God's Word. You know, Victory is the name of my church and victory is what I try to live out in my life no matter what, now. I'm determined to find a way to be victorious regardless of what's going on right now. I gave my life to the Lord, and now I make every effort to do what's right. I'm not perfect, but I'm forgiven and I'm a new man. What I went through was a learning experience, and I chalk it up to that. No hard feelings, no bad blood. I don't have time for that, my focus is to keep moving towards victory.

Everything I know now I only wish I'd known 50 years ago. But God knows why I needed to live this experience and go through this trial. I believe it's for the people reading my story. It was for you. All I can offer is my testimony and wisdom based on what I've seen and what I've lived. We all have choices to make, my hope is that, before you make any decision (whatever it may be), you count the cost. Is the quick money worth it? Because I can tell you, it wasn't. Don't be pressured by money or circumstances, have faith in God and do the right thing. I'm telling you; it will save you a lot of heartache. Fifty years ago, a man said this to me, "Son, the Lord can take away everything He gives you." I wish I'd paid more attention to what he was trying to tell me because now I know, firsthand, what he meant.

Made in the USA
Middletown, DE
07 September 2021